Prayers Plainly Spoken

STANLEY HAUERWAS

InterVarsity Press
Downers Grove, Illinois

InterVarsity Press
P.O. Box 1400, Downers Grove, IL 60515
World Wide Web: www.ivpress.com
E-mail: mail@ivpress.com

*InterVarsity Press® is the book-publishing division of InterVarsity Christian
Fellowship/USA®, a student movement active on campus at hundreds of universities,
colleges and schools of nursing in the United States of America, and a member
movement of the International Fellowship of Evangelical Students. For information
about local and regional activities, write Public Relations Dept., InterVarsity
Christian Fellowship/USA, 6400 Schroeder Rd., P.O. Box 7895, Madison, WI
53707-7895.*

Cover photograph: Tony Stone Images

ISBN 0-8308-2209-7

Printed in the United States of America ♾

Library of Congress Cataloging-in-Publication Data

Hauerwas, Stanley, 1940-
    Prayers plainly spoken / Stanley Hauerwas.
       p.   cm.
    ISBN 0-8308-2209-7 (pbk. : alk. paper)
    1. Prayers. I. Title.
BV245.H33   1999
242'.8—dc21   *99-18735*
                                                                              CIP

17 16 15 14 13 12 11 10 9 8 7 6 5 4 3 2 1

12 11 10 09 08 07 06 05 04 03 02 01 00 99

To Joel Adam
and his parents
Laura
and Adam

CONTENTS

Preface

I am in debt to the students at the divinity school at Duke University for allowing me to pray before my classes in Christian Ethics. I am grateful to those students (particularly the Reverend Jennifer Fitts) for urging me to make these prayers available beyond the classroom. Without such encouragement I would have never had the courage to venture out and publish these prayers. But then without Rodney Clapp I would have never known how to imagine this book; his skill and friendship made the book possible. As I will explain in the introduction, that I am able to pray at all is my wife Paula's "fault." I pray I will never take her love of God or me for granted. Both loves, in quite different ways, are extraordinary. It gives me great pleasure to dedicate this book to another set of loves, Joel Adam, Laura and Adam Hauerwas. I pray God will grant them challenging and good lives.

Introduction

At Hauerwas family gatherings my father was the "designated pray-er." At Thanksgivings, Christmases, Easters, wedding anniversaries and all other occasions when that large crew of five other uncles and their families would gather at my grandparents' house—at that moment just before we ate, my father would be asked to pray. Looking on with my many cousins, I was in awe that it fell on my father to "ask grace." I was not sure why this extraordinary task was assumed to be fulfilled only by my father, but there was no doubt that he was the chosen one. So pray he did, and I vaguely remember they were good, if quite similar, prayers.

Of course, we were a Southern family. In the South it was assumed someone in the family would be born with the gift of prayer. I do not know how my father was the one discovered to have this gift. By the time I came along, it was an assumed family fact. But I had no reason to doubt that my father was rightly chosen. After all, he prayed often at our family meals, particularly after church when the minister was invited over for fried chicken.

My problem began when I discovered that the gift of

prayer was assumed to be genetic. As my father's son I was to inherit the mantle of the "gift of prayer." It was one thing for it to be assumed, in the shadow of my father the bricklayer, that as a Hauerwas I would learn to lay brick. I liked that. I did not like the idea that I was to become the "pray-er."

For the truth of the matter is that I was no good at it. I just could not get the hang of praying. I was suddenly asked to be "pious" for thirty seconds. It always felt phony to me. After I was "called" to the ministry at fourteen (a call that for the good of the church never came to fruition), I still could not pray. Even after I had gone to seminary and later finished a Ph.D. in theology, I could not pray off-the-cuff. I understood that prayer is the heart of the Christian life, but I could not, so to speak, "pray on my own." It was one thing to pray the prayers of the church, which I found I could not live without. It was quite another thing to pray my own prayers.

Such was the state of things until I came to teach at Duke Divinity School. Paula Gilbert, now my wife, asked me if I prayed before class. I had never prayed before a class. Teaching undergraduates at Augustana College and the University of Notre Dame, it just did not seem appropriate. It was, of course, assumed that undergraduates at Notre Dame were Catholics, but even there I thought prayer before class could not help but be coercive. Yet I could find no excuse to offer Paula why a prayer should not be said before each class in a divinity school's core course in Christian ethics. So, obedient to her instruction that I should pray before class, I resolved to do so even though I did not like it. This book is the result of that resolve.

I knew that I lacked the depth required to pray "spontaneously." So each morning before the class I took time to write a prayer. I did not know what I was doing, but I was determined to do it. It was not long before students began asking me for copies of my prayers. I was not sure what to make of such requests, partly because I did not want to become overly self-conscious about what I was doing. After all, prayer should not call attention to itself, but rather to the one to whom we pray. Yet it was unmistakably clear that something I was doing when I prayed struck a chord in some of my students.

The students even began to ask me to publish these prayers, but I resisted that suggestion. Among the reasons I did not want to publish these prayers was the problem I have always had with prayer itself: I did not want to appear pious. Of course I have no reason to fear appearing pious, simply because I am not pious, or at least I do not manifest those forms of behavior that are usually associated with piety. I should like to think I have a due reverence for those people and things that are properly due reverence, but I do not try to be "holy." I fear "holiness" because in our time "holiness" is too often one of the ways the truthfulness of religious claims is lost.

Notice, for example, how in spite of our best intentions our attention wanders when someone "drops" into the pious tones and set formulas we associate with saying a prayer. That we find it hard to listen, I suspect, is because the "holiness" associated with prayer makes the attitude of prayer more important than the words we say. All that matters is someone is praying. As a result, prayer becomes an emotive exercise that only confirms our anthropocentric needs.

That these prayers are not "holy" is one of the reasons I suspect some of my students wanted them available to be read again. If anything, these prayers are plain. They are so because I discovered I could not pray differently than I speak. In other words, I thought it would be a mistake to try to assume a different identity when I prayed. I figured (Texans "figure") that God could take it because God did not need to be protected. I think I learned this over the years by praying the Psalms in church. God does not want us to come to the altar different from how we live the rest of our lives. Therefore I do not try to be pious or to use pious language in my prayers. I try to speak plainly, yet I hope with some eloquence, since nothing is more eloquent than simplicity.

On the Nature of These Prayers

It would be disingenuous of me, however, to pretend that what it means for these prayers to be "plain" is that they are not the result of "thought." I am a theologian. I have spent my life privileged to read Augustine, Aquinas, Luther, Calvin, Barth and, God help me, Wesley. If what I have learned from them—and from so many other Christians who may not have been theologians but lived wonderful Christian lives—does not make a difference in how I have learned to pray, I should be counted among the most ungrateful of God's creatures. False humility is no less false when feigned in the interest of being "just another Christian." I am "just another Christian," but I am also one who has been given certain responsibilities because of the gifts of time and learning the church has made available to me.

Of course it is also a very dangerous thing for a theologian to pray or, at least, write prayers for the church. Those with theological training may be tempted to write prayers that reflect their particular theological perspective or, perhaps even worse, to make or develop an argument. Such a temptation, of course, is but an indication of the peculiar character of modern theology. Modernity marks the time when theologians began to believe that their task is to explain the truth of what Christians believe in a manner that assumes the explanation is truer than the belief itself. Such theology is no longer the servant of the church but tries to be its master. That I have been critical of this theological project makes me no less subject to it, just to the extent that we too often become what we oppose.

That said, however, it is my hope that these prayers reflect what I have learned about what it means to be a Christian. I have had and I continue to have good teachers in prayer. I will be disappointed if those who have read some of my other work do not find some of what I think reflected in these prayers. Theology is the never-finished discipline of learning to speak with, to and about God. Prayer, accordingly, is our most determinative speech. Any theology, therefore, that is finally not about helping us to pray cannot be Christian. In an odd way, then, this book represents the most important testing of my theological work.

I hope many or even most people who read these prayers will be new to the work of Stanley Hauerwas. You do not need to know my "theological position" in order to read and hopefully to pray these prayers. It is my fervent desire that all anyone needs to pray these prayers is a common desire to worship the God found in Jesus Christ. Of course I would not object if some, on reading these prayers, are led to read other things I have written. But I certainly do not think that is necessary. If you need to know what I think to understand these prayers, then they are not prayers worth praying.

That most of these prayers were written to be prayed before a class, moreover, does not mean they are "academic."

It is true that they open a class in Christian ethics and that I did often write the prayers in relation to what we were studying in the class. But since the class is shaped by the liturgy of the church, I do not think the prayers are in any particular way limited to the interest of students and teachers. Whether in or out of a classroom, all our lives are marked by beginnings, endings and the "muddling through" that we do in between.[1]

So though most of the prayers were written with some reference to what we were studying on a particular day in the course (for instance, Scripture and preaching), they were also responses to events in the world and in our immediate community. Prayers were said in response to the outbreak of a war, the devastation of hurricane Fran, the suicide of one of our students, the deaths of a professorial colleague and parents of friends, and the betrayal of the seminary community by a faculty member.

These are examples enough to indicate that the "stuff" of these prayers is simply the stuff of life. And that should come as no surprise because the life of universities, and in particular seminaries, is constituted by the same invariables that shape all life: birth, faithfulness and unfaithfulness, truth and lies, forgiveness and blame, sex, peace, and violence, beauty and ugliness, youth and growing old, dying and death, and most important, God. All this, of course, is given form through our worship of God. That is why ethics is best taught liturgically.

I should add that not all of these prayers were written for the class. I have, for example, included one prayer I wrote when I was asked to pray in one of those awkward circum-

---

[1] I give an account of the way I teach Christian ethics in my book *In Good Company: The Church as Polis* (Notre Dame, Ind.: University of Notre Dame Press, 1995), pp. 153-68.

stances in which a Christian is to "return thanks," but you cannot pray to the Christian God because many people there are not Christian. I agreed to do this once, and my prayer "Addressing the God Who Is Not the Ultimate Vagueness" is the way I resolved the dilemma. I confess I do not think there is any satisfactory "solution," and I recommend that Christians no longer perform these rites of civil religion. A vague god vaguely prayed to serves no one well. I can report that because of my intervention (and perhaps, prayer) we no longer have a prayer at this event at my university. Instead we have a moment of silence.

If any one thing characterizes these prayers, I hope, as I noted above, it is a confidence that God wants our prayers and the prayers God wants are *our* prayers. We do not need to hide anything from God, which is a good thing given the fact that any attempt to hide from God will not work. God wants us to cry, to shout, to say what we think we understand and what we do not. The way we learn to do all this is by attending to the prayers of those who have gone before us. I try, therefore, to embed these prayers in the stories of our biblical forebears, believing that through them we discover that we have in fact become part of that great company that constitutes God's mighty prayer for the world.

Those stories, moreover, force us to discover ways of addressing God and thus describing our lives in ways otherwise unimaginable. I do not have the gifts or skills of the poet, but I am sure that prayer rightly forces us to discover speech otherwise undiscoverable. For example, the expression used in one of these prayers about prayer as "effortless work" came only through the discovery of the joy prayer makes possible. "Effortless work" sounds like a paradox if used to describe much of our life, but in reference to prayer it is a perfectly straightforward claim. I hope some who read these prayers will discover that the language of the prayers enriches their lives—because our lives finally are prayers. That hope is the only justification for publishing these prayers.

Prayers for Joel

The astute reader, however, will have noticed that I have not noted what immediate reason helped me decide, finally, to publish these prayers. The reason is named Joel Adam Hauerwas and was born on March 25, 1998, the Feast of the Annunciation. He is my grandson. I long to give him a gift that will in some way suggest the tradition into which he is born—that is, the church of Jesus Christ. In these uncertain times such a gift can be a desperate attempt to ensure that Joel's life will reflect the habits of a culture that assumed someone in the family necessarily had the gift of prayer. The problem with such desperation is that it belies the joy that makes us Christian. Of course I want Joel to be a Christian, but I am equally sure that I cannot guarantee that result.

Certainly that result will not come through Joel's knowing his grandfather was a theologian or even by reading my theology. Theology always bears too much the mark of "explanation." So: in further considering whether or not I should publish these prayers, it occurred to me that if I have anything to give Joel, it is these prayers.

These prayers are the best gift I can give my grandson exactly because they are not really mine. Rather, I hope they are "ours"—that they are the kinds of prayers Christians have learned to pray in times as strange as these. Joel will no doubt have to learn to pray differently than we have had to pray, but I hope he can learn something from these prayers toward that task. For what more could we ever ask or pray?

Part One
BEGINNINGS

Reborn and Unafraid

LORD OF THE FLOOD, wash us with your Spirit that we may be your ark of life, your peace in the sea of violence. Water is life; water cleans; water kills. Frightened, we are tempted to make a permanent home on the ark. But you force us to seek dry ground. We can do so only because you have taught us to cling to our baptisms, where we are drowned and reborn by the water and fire of your Spirit. So reborn, make us unafraid. AMEN.

Are We Yet Alive, Lord?

ARE WE YET ALIVE, LORD? We feel pain, sorrow, happiness. We cry, wail, laugh. Are these signs that we are alive? Or are they but death-gurgles masquerading as signs of life? We find it hard to believe, to understand, that we come to life through being baptized into your Son's good death. Yet you have made us your baptized, giving us life, life that makes our pain, sorrow and happiness real. Life that makes our crying, wailing and laughing service to one another. Raise us, then, from our watery graves shouting, "Jesus Christ is Lord!" so that the world may see your liveliness, your love. AMEN.

Who Am I to Pray?

GRACIOUS GOD, we thank you for the gift of prayer. What an extraordinary thing that we can pray to you, unburden ourselves before you, place our cares, woes and joys before you. I confess I find praying an awkward business. I keep thinking, *Who am I to pray?* But I know that to be false humility, hiding my prideful desire to be my own creator. So we pray a prayer of joy in prayer, asking that we become your prayers for one another. AMEN.

Teach Me to Beg

DEAR JESUS, send your Spirit on us so that we will be taught to pray. Prayer is hard, requiring great effort, but when done, effortless. I confess I have never liked to pray. Prayer is too much like begging. So I have to pray that your generous Spirit will teach me to beg. I beg you to help all of us discover that our lives are constituted by prayer, so that we may be in your world one mighty, joyous prayer. Make us so rested by such prayer, so content to be your people, that we kill no more. AMEN.

Lives Built on Past Murders

*I wrote this prayer during the celebration of the five hundredth
anniversary of Columbus's "discovery" of America.*

DEAR GOD, our lives are made possible by the
murders of the past—civilization is built on slaugh-
ters. Acknowledging our debt to killers frightens
and depresses us. We fear judging, so we say,
"That's in the past." We fear to judge because in
so judging we are judged. Help us, however, to
learn to say no, to say, "Sinners though we are, that
was and is wrong." May we do so with love. AMEN.

Save Us from Dullness

OUR ONLY FATHER, humble us Mary-like before the cross of your Son, our Lord, Jesus of Nazareth, so that through the Spirit we may be joined in the one body, the church, thus becoming your one mighty prayer for the world. Gracious God, whose grace terrorizes and sustains us, we pray for courage as we begin this course. Invade our lives, robbing us of fear and envy so we might begin to trust one another and in the process discover a bit of the truth. In this serious business grant us the joy and humor that comes from your presence. And for your sake, save us from being dull. AMEN.

Make Us Like Him

SPIRIT OF TRUTH, direct our attention to the life of Jesus so that we might see what you would have us be. Make us, like him, teachers of your good law. Make us, like him, performers of miraculous cures. Make us, like him, proclaimers of your kingdom. Make us, like him, loving of the poor, the outcast, children. Make us, like him, silent when the world tempts us to respond in the world's terms. Make us, like him, ready to suffer. We know we cannot be like Jesus except as Jesus was unlike us, being your Son. Make us cherish that unlikeness, that we may grow into the likeness made possible by Jesus' resurrection. AMEN.

Confronted with Lovely Lives

Wanda Camp was, for many years, the executive secretary to the religion department at Duke. She was one of the those wonderful people on whom universities depend but whose importance is too often taken for granted. She battled cancer for a number of years with the courage and good humor you would expect given her membership in the church of Christ.

GOD, how we pray that you will make our ordinary lives extraordinary. We fear the anonymity, the ordinary promises. We want to force others to remember us by being more than we are. But then you confront us with lovely lives like that of Wanda Camp—lives lived in service, lives lived in joy. We are saddened by her death but rejoice that the communion of your saints is enriched by that wiry little ball of energy. Help us live as she lived, seeking to be no more than one of your servants in service to others. Thank you for such lives. AMEN.

Living Confessions of Love

LORD OF ALL LIFE, we come before you not knowing who we are. We strut our stuff, trying to impress others with our self-confidence. In the process we hope to be what we pretend. Save us from such pretense, that we might learn who we are through trust in you to make us more than we can imagine. Help us, Augustine-like, to reread our lives as confessions of sin made possible by your love. Bind up our wounds and our joys so that our lives finally make sense only as a prayer to you. AMEN.

Give Us the Sight of Children

LIGHT OF TRUE LIGHT, true God from true God, give us clear sight, courage to see your sinful, rebellious, dreadful world as it is, not as we want it to be. Save us from narcissistic fascinations that cloud our understanding with our unknowings. Give us clear and innocent sight, the sight of children, capable of seeing beauty in a common rock. Your creation glows with your fiery glory. Draw us to the fire, consume us with your glory, that we may glow with your salvation, your light for the world. AMEN.

All the Time in the World

END OF ALL OUR BEGINNINGS, Lord of time, who alone makes time a gift, remind us we are creatures with a beginning. We confess we often forget we are your timeful creatures. We fear the forgetfulness our death beckons. We are driven frantically to work, thinking we can ensure we will not be forgotten, ensure our own place in time. How silly we must look to you, ants building anthills to no purpose. Help us take joy and rest in your time, eucharistic time, a time redeemed through Jesus' resurrection, that we can rest easy in our dying. You have given us all the time in the world. May we take pleasure in it. AMEN.

Adrift at Sea, Thank God

LORD OF THE WATERS, you have set us adrift in a trackless ocean, in a leaky boat with no oars or rudder. "Rudderless" nicely describes our situation, but matters are worse. Even if we had a rudder, we would not know which direction to go. We are not even sure if there are any directions—or if there are any directions, we so distrust our wants that we do not know which way we really want to go. In short, we feel lost and, so feeling, think it is probably your fault. Yet you refuse to let us drown in self-pity and blame. Instead you drown us in your good kingdom, the death and resurrection of Jesus our Lord, making us part of that great ark, your church. The winds of your love blow that ark out to sea, away from the shores we think might provide safety, so that we might take on board the drowning. How wonderful it is that the more that are taken on board, the less your ark is crowded and the safer we are. Thank you for making us steady sailors who have no reason to fear the unknown, having learned you would have us be at sea. AMEN.

Courage for the Journey

LORD OF TIME, end of all our beginnings, make the beginning of this course part of your purpose. Make us rejoice that we cannot create our own beginnings. Help us discover even through this course that we have been made participants in your purpose—called kingdom. As citizens of that kingdom, force us to recognize our need for one another, and in that humiliating recognition may we discover the humility to acknowledge truthfully that which is true. We confess as we begin this course that we are a bit frightened, probably not so much by you as by our own inadequacies. I know I am frightened, because I have to act like I know what I am doing, since I am supposed to change these students' lives and in the process even have my life changed. I do not like to change, but at least when all is said and done, I know that it is your fault that we, students and teacher alike, are so caught. Give us the good humor that comes from being forced into this strange and weird world of yours. Give us courage as we embark on this journey, that we will want to know the truth about ourselves. Help us remember that when all is said and done, you are in the beginning because you are the end. AMEN.

Part Two
LIVING
IN BETWEEN

Lies We Wrap in Love

DEAR GOD, we often ask you to invade our lives, to plumb the secrets of our hearts unknown even to ourselves. But in fact we do not desire that. What we really want to scream, if only to ourselves, is "Do not reveal to us who we are!" We think we are better people if you leave us to our illusions. Yes, we know another word for a life of illusion is *hell*. But we are surrounded by many caught up in such a hell—people too deficient of soul even to be capable of lying, but only of self-deceit. Dear God, we ask your mercy on all those so caught, particularly if we are among them. The loneliness of such a life is terrifying. Remind us, compel us to be truthful, painful as that is. For without the truth, without you, we die. Save us from the pleasantness which too often is but a name for ambition. Save us from the temptation to say to another what we think she wants to hear rather than what we both need to hear. The regimen of living your truth is hard, but help us remember that any love but truthful love is cursed. The lie wrapped in love is just another word for violence. For God's sake, for the world's sake, give us the courage and the love to speak truthfully, so that we might be at peace with one another and with you. AMEN.

Thanksgiving for Armadillos and Custodians

HOW EXTRAORDINARY it is that you, God of Mary's womb, never tire of your creation. We praise you, we thank you, for making us alive through your exuberant creation. Thank you for creating a world so full of color (particularly lime green), so full of difference (such as armadillos), so full of magic (such as your Word and sacraments). The wonder of it all saves us from our narcissistic presumptions that everything finally all depends on us. Thank you also for giving us in the midst of the wonder of it all good work to do, that we might be of service to one another. As those whose work it is to read and write, we give you particular thanks for Annie, who cleans my office, and for Jean, Dawn, Cedric, Sylvester, Lessie and Donald, all of the housekeeping staff, who do the work necessary to give us the space and time to study. The wonder of the kindness of their lives humbles us. May our work witness their wonderful lives. AMEN.

The Good Work of Praise

STRANGE LORD, who would rule your creation through the crucified Son of a carpenter, make us workers in your kingdom. We want to work, but so often our work turns out to be nothing but busyness. We think that if we are busy we must be doing something that you can use. At least being busy hides our boredom. Yet we know you would not have us busy, having given us the good work of prayer. Help us, in our busyness, learn to pray— so that all our work, all that is our lives, may glorify you. In a world that for so many seems devoid of purpose, we praise you for giving us the good work of praise. HALLELUJAH AND AMEN.

God, Could You Leave Us Alone?

ZEALOUS GOD, we confess, like your people Israel, that we tire of being "the chosen." Could you not just leave us alone every once in a while? Sometimes this "Christian stuff" gets a bit much. Life goes on and we have lives to live. Yet, unrelenting, you refuse to leave us alone. You are, after all, a zealous God. You startle us from our reveries by gathering us into your dream time, into your church. May we, thus gathered, be so inspired by your Spirit that our lives never tire, that we have the energy now to wait, to rest, in the goodness and beauty of your truth. AMEN.

The Ridiculous World

HOLY ONE OF ISRAEL, who called Abraham and Sarah out of Ur, who called us, your church, out of the nations, save us from self-righteousness. You have made us different so that our difference might save the world. But too often our difference tempts us to ridicule because the world, after all, is ridiculous. Never let us forget that we too are the world, and so also ridiculous. Shape the judgments of our neighbors and our own foolish judgments by your love, so that we might be together saved—that is, be a people that continue the journey out of Ur. AMEN.

Violate Them with Your Terrible Grace

GOD, we are angry and frightened. We know you created us for peace, but our world is just so violent. Two of our community have been violated. One beaten, the other raped. Dear God, this is not supposed to happen. Not here at a university. Not here among the privileged. So we are angry and frightened. We ask your comfort for those violated. We ask your justice for those whose souls are so numb they cannot feel the pain they inflict. They need you most of all. Violate them with your terrible grace, that they may feel again. And make us your peace; rob us of the violence of our privileges, that we may be a refuge so that such evil can come to an end. AMEN.

Addressing the God Who Is Not the "Ultimate Vagueness"

The call came from the president's office asking me to pray before the Distinguished Professor's luncheon. Reynolds Price, the distinguished novelist and member of the English department at Duke, was to give the presentation that day. Since I have harshly and repeatedly criticized civil religion, I at first turned down the opportunity to pray to a vague God who cannot be named as the Father of Jesus Christ. I knew such a "public" occasion, involving people of many faiths, would have people expecting just such a civil religious address of God. But then I reconsidered and called back saying I would do it. It took me all morning to write the prayer. I describe the results in the introduction to this volume.

GOD, you alone know how we are to pray to you on occasions like this. We do not fear you, since we prefer to fear one another. Accordingly, our prayers are not to you but to some "ultimate vagueness." You have, of course, tried to scare the hell out of some of us through the creation of your people Israel and through the life, death and resurrection of Jesus. But we are a subtle, crafty and stiff-necked people who prefer to be damned into vagueness. So we thank you for giving us common gifts such as food, friendship and good works that remind us our lives are gifts made possible by sacrifice. We are particularly grateful for your servant Reynolds Price, who graces our lives with your grace. Through such gifts may our desire for status and the envy status breeds be transformed into service that glorifies you. AMEN.

Free Us from Self-Fascination

LORD ALMIGHTY, we say we want to serve you, we say we want to help others less fortunate than ourselves, we say we want justice. But the truth is, we want power and status because we so desperately need to be loved. Free us from our self-fascination and the anxious activity it breeds, so that we might be what we say we want to be—loved by you and thus capable of unselfish service. AMEN.

Faltering Rulers

MASTER OF THE UNIVERSE, you have made us your servants, kings and queens in your world. We confess we do not feel much like rulers: we are not only incapable of doing what we want, we are not even sure what we should or do want. We, in short, do not even seem to rule ourselves. As a result we fail you, our brothers and sisters in Christ, our brothers and sisters who are in the world, and ourselves. Give us the enthusiasm of your Spirit, that we may be so filled with your love that others will be attracted to your rule. As those ruled by you, may we witness how service can govern. AMEN.

The Only True Time

LORD OF TIME, who became time by calling Abraham and Sarah to be our forebears, we confess we are not sure we are ready for all this. Our lives so often feel like the meandering of those lost in a wood so thick we cannot even tell when we recross our previous trails. We undo what was done and then complain we have no past, nothing gained. We are so busy, but we fear our busyness is but a distraction necessary to hide from ourselves that we are lost and do not know where we are. Help us to take time to rest, confident that the time created by Christ's resurrection is our only true time. Grant us serenity. AMEN.

Saved by God's Entertainment

DEAR GOD, who saves by entertaining us with the magic of your kingdom, help us to know and thus be your magic so we can be instruments of your peace. You give us life, wonderful enthralling life, that grows through dispossession. Help us to know that the life you give is not a zero-sum game, that love cannot be used up but rather increases with its sacrifice. How wonderful it is to be your people. AMEN.

Worthy Agents of Your Peace

SAVING GOD, free us from hardness of heart, take from us all pride and pretension, strip us clean of all that makes us incapable of being witnesses of your gentle love. Make us worthy agents of your peace, so that even as we contend with one another the world may say, "But see how they love one another." AMEN.

Theology as a Way to Control You

REVEALING AND TERRIFYING GOD, whose very revelation is mystery, forgive our frightened attempts to possess you. You have created us for yourself, but we find that hard to believe, much less live. So we strut across your creation as if we really understood you. Theology becomes our way to try to be in control, dear God, even of you. So we ask for the humility that comes from the unavoidable recognition that you insist on our being your people. What an extraordinary thing. AMEN.

Fierce and Friendly Lord . . .

FIERCE AND FRIENDLY LORD, we feel alone, but even here in school and in this class we discover friends we did not know we had. The discovery that we are not alone both gladdens and frightens us. Sharing life threatens loss of self. Give us the grace to learn that we have no life not shared. Father, Son and Holy Spirit, make us in your image so that we might be worthy witnesses of the joy that comes from your claiming us as friends. AMEN.

Thank You for Unsettling Our Lives

ALMIGHTY GOD, whose Mary-like beauty compels our attention, give us hearts that jump within us with the good news of your salvation. We confess that amidst the tedium of the everyday our worship of you sometimes feels like a job—just "one more thing." Thank you for the unsettling of our lives, wherein we discover the splendor of the kingdom made possible by your Son, Jesus Christ. We pray that you will ever be here, unsettling our attempts to domesticate the wildness of your Spirit. AMEN.

A Plea for Peace with Chickens

SOVEREIGN OF ALL LIFE, we pray that you will give us the patience to stay still long enough to witness the beauty of your creation. Help us live at peace with your world, especially with our brothers and sisters in and without the church. Help us to live at peace with those creatures not like us—that is, dogs, pigs and even, God help us, chickens. And help us to live in peace with ourselves. AMEN.

Your Unrelenting (and Tiresome) Presence

DEAR GOD, we confess that often we find your unrelenting presence tiresome. It is so hard to live seemingly caught between what it seems you want us to be and what we know we are. Help us to realize that our very pretensions of unworthiness are unworthy. Make us glad to be your people, gathered into your church, celebrating the victory that is ours. AMEN.

Virtues of Fear and Hate

GOD OF LIGHT, shine in our darkness that we may see that this world, for all its distortion by sin, is still your world. Give us the virtue of courage to fear rightly that which we should rightly fear. Give us the virtue of love that we might rightly hate that which is hateful. Give us the virtue of prudence that we might know what to fear and hate. For this task we pray that we might learn to trust one another, as we are incapable of being faithful alone. AMEN.

Make Us Visible, Make Us Real

INVISIBLE GOD, by the power of your love you make present the bodies of the invisible, the poor, the farm worker, the foreigner, the dead. Assault us with such presence, as through them you promise to give us your presence. Make us visible; make us real. Make us capable of feeling so we may think. Make us capable of tears so we may laugh. Make us your visible people, your light, your joy. AMEN.

Sheep Gathered from the Slaughter

MASTER OF THE UNIVERSE, there is no place so large or so small that it escapes your direction. We thank you for creating the space you have taught us to call church. You have gathered us as sheep from the slaughter so that the world might know that slaughter is not our nature or destiny. Make us friends with one another, and in that befriending may we know your truth. AMEN.

A Prayer to the Jester King

FUNNY LORD, Jester King, you are surely a strange God. You must have an extraordinary sense of humor to trust your kingdom to a people like us. That you have done so, however, makes us happy—giddy with the confidence that comes from being brought together to share in the adventure of your kingdom. Make us as lively and entertaining as your Spirit so that others may be attracted to the wonder of your creation. AMEN.

Thanksgiving for Those Who Preceded Us

OUR FATHER, you who have mothered us by giving us good forebears, we thank you for those who have preceded us. Without them, faithful and unfaithful, we would not be. Often we little understand what they must have been like, yet they passed on to us a sense of how wonderful it is to be your people. May we be capable of producing yet new generations born of your hope. AMEN.

Humble Us Through the
Violence of Your Love

GRACIOUS GOD, humble us through the violence of your love so we are able to know and confess our sins. We want our sins to be interesting, but, God forgive us, they are so ordinary: envy, hatred, meanness, pride, self-centeredness, laziness, boredom, lying, lust, stinginess and so on. You have saved us from "and so on" to be a royal people able to witness to the world that the powers that make us such ordinary sinners have been defeated. So capture our attention with the beauty of your life that the ugliness of sin may be seen as just that— ugly. God, how wonderful it is to be captivated by you. AMEN.

A Prayer for Defeated Enemies

HUMBLED LORD, give us the grace not to exult over the defeat of your enemies. We confess that we do not possess the humility for that feat, so you will have to help us. Injuries are real, and we often want to destroy those who injure in the name of righteousness. You have called us to be your peaceable people. We do not like it, but help us live it and in the living learn to love you. AMEN.

We Play at Being Faithful

ORIGIN OF ALL RIGHTEOUSNESS, confronted by you we confess our unworthiness, even our sin. It is a terrible thing to be so found by you. We want you to like us, and so we try to hide who we are. We play at being faithful. Alas, such play only becomes an occasion for more sin. Yet you forgive us in a way that does not destroy. You make us your own and in the process free us from our enjoyment of our sin. It is good to be forgiven by you. AMEN.

The Presumptuous Confession of Sin

GRACIOUS GOD, forgive us our presumptions to confess our sin. Only your favor makes it possible for us to know and acknowledge our sins. But that same grace heals as it wounds, and for that we are grateful. Lead us beyond fascination with our sin into the wonder of friendship with you and one another. AMEN.

Make Us Attentive to Your Words

WORD OF ALL WORDS, source of all worth knowing, make us attentive to your words. We thank you for making us a people of the book, a people who know that insofar as we live, we live by memory, in your memory. Never let us forget the saints who have died that we may live. Through them we hear and live your Word and thus are graced. How wonderful it is to be your servants. AMEN.

The Simplicity to Be Confounded

GREAT GOD, humble us so that we will be capable of hearing your Word. We thank you for the gift of yourself in the Scripture. We rejoice in its complexity. Give us the simplicity to be confounded by your Word. AMEN.

Make Us Children

LORD OF ALL WISDOM, we thank you for your Word, Jesus Christ. Illumine our minds and bodies by that Word so that we might see every part of your creation as a reflection of your glory. In particular help us not miss the small and contingent rocks, plants and animals in which children so delight. Make us children, so that we might enjoy the sheer giftedness of your creation. AMEN.

Save Us from Abusing Your Power

FOR CHRIST'S SAKE, God, give us the strength to be your servants. We are ministers of your gospel, called to service, but we confess we fear the power you bestow on us to be able so to serve. Help us, therefore, be servants of your joy, as through joy are we freed from coercion and violence of the everyday. We thank you for making us representative of your kingdom. AMEN.

Save Us from False Ambition

GOD, I am just too busy. Too many people, too many questions, too much to do. We confess we stay busy because we fear acknowledging our emptiness. How amid this busyness do we rest? How do we worship you? Please create space, which may be other people, to make time, our time, serve you. Force us to rest through the activity of prayer so that all our loves and fears might be made perfect in you. Help us see how such busy service, if it is service, may be just the rest we need—just the worship we need. Finally, and most importantly, save us from false ambition. AMEN.

The Lustiness of Your Kingdom

LOVELY AND COMPELLING GOD, draw us to your beauty so that our lives will glow with reverence for you. We confess that too often, if we glow at all, we are hot with hate and lust. We cannot will our lives free of these powers, so we ask that you send us faithful friends to transform our hate and lust to love. We rejoice in our bodies, for you would not have us be ethereal. Make us bold bodily lovers so that others might be drawn to the lustiness of your kingdom. AMEN.

A Prayer on Election Day

SOVEREIGN LORD, foolish we are, believing that we can rule ourselves by selecting this or that person to rule over us. We are at it again. Help us not to think it more significant than it is, but also give us and those we elect enough wisdom to acknowledge our follies. Help us laugh at ourselves, for without humor our politics cannot be humane. We desire to dominate and thus are dominated. Free us, dear Lord, for otherwise we perish. AMEN.

Your Unrelenting Hospitality

DEAR GOD, you alone know the loneliness and thus the terror of our lives. Indeed you know us better than we can know ourselves. Give us your knowledge of us so that we might not be so alone. Be with those who seem simply lost, abandoned, alienated from friends and from you. Heal us with your unrelenting hospitality, so that we are capable of breaking through the splendid isolation we create, which we call freedom and power. Help us to be touched and be able to touch without violence. We know that is possible only because you have touched us with the body and blood of your Son. Thank you for that. AMEN.

Not Certainty, but Joy

TRUE GOD OF ALL TRUTHS, how we desire certainty amid the confusion of our lives. We think we could make it if we just had one thing we could know without doubt, one way to be that was not ambiguous, one other we could unreservedly trust. Yet all such knowledge, being and trust too often reflect our desperation rather than your glory. We pray, therefore, not for certainty but for joy at the discernment that you have discovered us and given us a way to go on in the midst of confusion. For what more could we ask? AMEN.

The Audacity of Commitment

A prayer I offer before I lecture on marriage in the Christian ethics course.

UNRELENTING GOD, your faithfulness is fearful to us. We desire a love more occasional, more spontaneous, less serious. Even worse, you call us to be unrelenting lovers—capable of making lifelong promises like "until death do us part." Such a vow is surely a miracle, since only you can give us the boldness to so pledge ourselves. We thank you for such audacity and pray that we may be faithful to one another as you have been to us. AMEN.

The Truth That Reveals Lies

GOD OF MIGHTY TRUTH, make us people of true speech, obedient speech, so that through our lives you may be revealed to others. We live in a world overcome by words that lie—but without words there is no truth. Work in us so that our words may be disciplined by your Word and the lies may be revealed. As those called to ministry, give us the courage to trust you, knowing you would never call a people to you who would prefer lies to truth. AMEN.

Children as Gospel

DEAR GOD, our children are wonderful news: the news that you refuse to give up on your creation. Against the blackness of this world, against the injustice, against the violence, against the busyness spurred by our inflated sense of importance, you give us children. What a wonderful gift. We thank you for Adam, Sarah Austin, Katie, Gabriel, Joshua Paul, Andrew Thomas, Joel and others. Thank you for these your children, who screw up our lives, thus teaching us our true desires. Like your Son, they are our fleshly advents, because through them we learn patient hope. Thank you for making us your joyful, confident children, capable of welcoming our children, hopefully in imitation of your welcome of us. AMEN.

Ferocious God, We Fear Your Peace

FEROCIOUS GOD, we fear your peace. We say we want peace, but we confess that war and violence capture our imagination and our spirits. Violate our violence with the transforming power of your love. Wrench us from all hatreds and loves that are the breeding ground of our violence. We cannot will that your peace come, but through the Spirit you make it possible for us to live in your peace. So fire us with that Spirit that the world might be flooded with your reconciling kingdom. AMEN.

Mercy for the War-Dead

DEAR LORD, at our feet lie dead Iraqis, dead Kuwaitis, dead Kurds, dead Croats, dead Slavs, dead Salvadorans, dead Americans, dead Palestinians, dead Israelis, dead Jews, dead children, dead Christians—dead, dead, dead. We ask your mercy on these war-dead sisters and brothers. We ask for the same mercy for ourselves, for our failure to be your peace, to be the end of war. Save us from the powers that capture our imagination so that we think our only alternative is war. We know we cannot will our way to peace, for when we try we end up fighting wars for peace. So compel us with your love that we might be your peace, thus bringing life to this deadly world. AMEN.

Do We Really Have to Make This Trip?

This prayer was written to begin the section of the Christian ethics course on "Sending Forth."

GOD OF ABRAHAM, Sarah, Isaac, Rebekah, Jacob, Ruth and Mary, you have called us through your Son, Jesus Christ. You lead us on our way by the fiery cloud of your Spirit. We ask you, "Do we really have to make this trip?" We are just beginning to get the hang of this "worship-of-God business," and then you tell us we have to go and we are not even sure there is anywhere to go to. Help us remember, as Hugo of St. Victor put it, "the man who finds his homeland sweet is still a tender beginner; he to whom every soil is as his native one is already strong; but he is perfect to whom the world is a foreign place." So we will go to travel the world. Help us remember we do not and cannot go alone. You have made us your friends and friends of one another. Help us trust in that friendship, knowing we will need it as you encounter us in the unknown. God, it is exhilarating to be your people. We praise you for giving us such wonderful work. AMEN.

No Rose Garden, but How About Some Daisies?

I wrote this prayer in response to a particularly egregious act by a member of the divinity school community that brought shame on the school.

WEIRD LORD, you never promised us a rose garden, but right now we could use a few daisies or zinnias. We feel confused, unsure of where we are, angry because a wrong has been done, and we are unsure who to blame. It ought to be somebody's fault, but even the one who is to blame is so pathetic it hardly seems worth the effort. So we are left with ourselves. Work on us to make us a community of truthfulness, a community where friendships flourish, a community of joy in the good work you have given us. Help us to know how to go on, confident that you have made us characters in the best story since creation, since it *is* the story of creation. It is good to be your

people. AMEN.

Life Is Sweet When We Are in Love

LOVING LORD, where would we be without friends? We would literally be no place. Alone in your creation, yet unable to recognize it as creation. It would just be another lonely place. But you place us next to one another, and being so placed we are forced to recognize that others exist. Bodies. Attraction. Recognition. Friendship. Love. How wonderful and frightening. We are not alone. You created us passionate beings hungry for one another. You want to make us your friends, and in that doing make us friends of one another and even ourselves. Life is sweet when we are in love. Praise you for giving us one another. AMEN.

Give Us Hope So We Can Wait

INVADE OUR BODIES with your hope, dear Lord, that we might manifest the enthusiasm of your kingdom. Give us the energy of children, whose lives seem fired by the wonder of it all. Thank God, you have given us good work, hopeful work. Our lives are not just one pointless thing after another. We have purpose. But give us also your patience. School our hope with humility, recognizing that finally it is a matter of your will being done. Too often our hope turns to optimism, optimism to despair, despair to cynicism. Save our hope by Israel-like patience so that we can learn to wait hopefully in joy. Surely that is why you give us children—signs of hope requiring infinite patience. Give us hope so we can learn to wait. Christ has died, Christ is risen, Christ will come again. AMEN.

Our Envy of the Jews

A prayer on Yom Kippur.

MASTER OF THE UNIVERSE, One of infinite energy, today you celebrate with your people Israel the birthday of your creation—their creation, made new through repentance and the rebirth of holiness. As Christians, dear Lord, we ask you to forgive us the sorry and terrifying persecution of your people. It is hard to control our envy. Humble us, restrain our hate, make us holy through repentance, that we might be pulled into your future, Christian and Jew, joined in common love of you. AMEN.

The Joy and Terror of Routine

THANK YOU, GOD, for giving us ordinary lives. We love the joy that comes from routine. The time you give us to eat breakfast, to come to class, to study, is wonderful. Help us not to forget the terror that surrounds us as well as dwells within the routine. I eat my bagel while some not far from me starve. I think I would have it otherwise, but I do not know how to have it otherwise. And in my helplessness I willfully forget the starving so I can enjoy my bagel. Help us remember. Help us know how to share so that the nourishing routines of your kingdom may be known to all. AMEN.

Stuck with a God Who Bleeds

BLOODY LORD, you are just too real. Blood is sticky, repulsive, frightening. We do not want to be stuck with a sacrificial God who bleeds. We want a spiritual faith about spiritual things, things bloodless and abstract. We want sacrificial spirits, not sacrificed bodies. But you have bloodied us with your people Israel and your Son, Jesus. We fear that by being Jesus' people we too might have to bleed. If such is our destiny, we pray that your will, not ours, be done. AMEN.

Fragmented People

HOLY LORD, we come before you fragmented people. Our lives are divided into pieces and we are unsure if the pieces when added up make up a life. What we do here, with one part of our life, seems undone there, with another part of our life. Who am I, Lord, who prays to you in this prayer? Where are we, Lord, when we so pray to you? Augustine has taught us we are restless until we find our rest in you, but this does not feel like such divine "restlessness"—it just feels confusing. Holy Lord, make us one with ourselves and one another. Form the scattered bits of our lives, the fragments of desires, into lives capable of saying "From the beginning you, dear God, were with me." Help us be capable of truthful memory and fervent hope so that our lives will reflect the purposefulness of your kingdom. So reflected, may our lives manifest for one another your holiness and the world may say, "They are God's people. See how they love one another." AMEN.

Help Us Cry for Help

BLESSED TRINITY, you gather us so that we will not be alone. You will us to enjoy one another, to rejoice in one another's existence. Just as you can be three, perfectly sharing but without loss of difference, so you make us capable of love without fear that in our love we will be lost. Yet we do find ways to be alone, to be in hell. Caught up in fantasies that we can create ourselves, we become frozen in our self-imposed smiles of self-satisfaction. Because we can fool others into believing we are in control, we even come to believe it ourselves. Great and powerful Lord, shake us free of such loneliness that we may cry for help and be surprised by the willingness of your people to share. How happy we are to be your people. AMEN.

Your Saints Are a Funny Lot

MARY-BORN LORD, humble us so that we also might say, "Let it be with me according to your word." We are tempted to will our way to humility because we just do not trust you with your creation. Someone has to make this world come out right. Thank you for surrounding us with your saints, whose lives remind us what your work looks like. Your saints are such a funny lot—weird and wonderful. They often make us laugh, Sarah-like, and through laughter we discover humility. God, it is wonderful to be made part of your entertainment so that the world might be freed from sin. AMEN.

I Do Not Want My Enemies Forgiven

FORGIVING LORD, I do not want my enemies forgiven. I want you to kill them (as sometimes prays the psalmist!). Actually, I would prefer to pray that you punish them rather than kill them, since I would like to watch them suffer. Also, I fear losing my enemies, since my hates are more precious to me than my loves. If I lost my hates, my enemies, how would I know who I am? Yet you have bent us toward reconciliation, that we may be able to pass one another Christ's peace. It is a terrible thing to ask of us. I am sure I cannot do it, but you are a wily God able to accomplish miracles. May we be struck alive with the miracle of your grace, even to being reconciled with ourselves. AMEN.

Can't We Just Be "Mildly Disliked"?

GOD OF JUSTICE AND MIGHT, we often pray that you will shelter us, protect us—from what we are not sure. After all, when you are people as nice as we are, it is hard to remember that as your people we are meant to have enemies. Your Scripture even suggests we are going to be hated. We confess that seems a little extreme. Can't we just be "mildly disliked"? So we must pray to you to send us keen sight, just seeing, that we might know our enemies and in that recognition engage them with the weapons of your Spirit. Give us the courage for that task, and please, dear Lord, like Luther's beloved chicken, protect us under your wings. AMEN.

Thank You for Making Us Thankful

THANK YOU, LORD, for making us thankful. We thank you for life itself; for the energy your passion for your creation gives us; for friendships through which we discover our lives; for love and lust that remind us we are bodies; for that body called the church, where our bodies are enlarged; for the Eucharist, the great thanksgiving, in which we are made part of your redemption. For all this we thank you. AMEN.

When Theology Is Noise

IN THE BEGINNING you created through your Word. You created us with language, giving us life, giving us prayer, giving us thought. Make all our thinking, jumbled as it is, prayer, so that we may be brought back to the quiet love, the eloquent silence, of your creation. So often we use your words to make noise to hide from ourselves our beginning. We call such noise theology. Humble us so that our presumption to think with and about you will be of service to one another, your church, and for the upbuilding of your kingdom. Please teach us to pray so we might speak. AMEN.

God's Joke on the World

FUNNY LORD, how we love this life you have given us. Of course we get tired, bored, worn down by the stupidity that surrounds us. But then that stupid person does something, says something that is wonderful, funny, insightful. How we hate for that to happen. But, thank God, you have given us one another, ensuring we will never be able to get our lives in order. Order finally is no fun, and you are intent on forcing us to see the humor of your kingdom. I mean really, Lord, the Jews! But there you have it. You insist on being known through such a funny people. And now us—part of your joke on the world. Make us your laughter. Make us laugh, and in the laughter may the world be so enthralled by your entertaining presence that we lose the fear that fuels our violence. Funny Lord, how we love this life you have given us. AMEN.

Thank You for Making Us Hungry

A prayer that begins the section of the course "Shaped by the Eucharist."

FESTIVE FATHER, you created us hungry. We must eat to live. And eating is a necessary habit, a wonderful reminder that we are, after all, creatures. But even more wonderful, you gave us your Son to be the host of the great meal, the glorious celebration of your peaceable kingdom. It is a meal of pain. It is a meal of unbounded joy. In our eating you story us. Give our eating purpose, make us participants in your unending sacrifice for all your creation. Thank you for making us hungry. May we eat in peace. AMEN.

Living Puzzles and the Kingdom of God

ALL PRAISE TO YOU, Father of our Lord, Jesus Christ, who Spirits your church into being, making us members one of another. It is a great mystery that we are your body. But we praise you for it, for otherwise we would be so alone—condemned to live alone, to die alone. But you have given us one another in all shapes and sizes. We do not fit together all that well, but we pray that the puzzles of our lives may please you and entertain you, so that in the end we add up to be your kingdom. Help us to live with the confidence of that kingdom, in the light of your Son's resurrection, so that when all is said and done, this may be said: "They were a strange lot, but look how they loved one another." AMEN.

Create in Us a Passion for Truth

TRUE GOD OF TRUE GOD, create in us a passion for truth. Make us lust for, long for, taste, feel, roll in the grass of your love, your truth. Free us from the fear of truth by making us God-fearers. May we hate all that which would tempt us to settle for the greatest of all lies, the half-truth. So formed, give us simple speech, graceful speech, lovely speech, so that we might truthfully speak to one another, that we might love one another in truth. Honor us with honesty that we might be honorable and, thus, trustworthy people. Oh! We so long to be capable of trust. We are so tired, so bored, by our cynicism. So yes, dear Lord, we pray that you will make us truthful servants so that we may say to ourselves and one another, "You can trust me." AMEN.

Do Not Rob Me of Anger

DEAR LORD, I am filled with anger born of frustration. I confess I know not whether all my anger is of you. I just know I am filled with hope, which makes me angry that others are not so filled. Take away the self-aggrandizing righteousness that so often accompanies such anger, but please do not rob me of the anger. It is energy. Make it to be of service. Help me pass it on. We are taught by the world to fear anger. Yet we know that you are a just judge, angry because we are not justly angry. We want you to be like us—get along by going along. You will not play that game. You expect your church to be faithful—yes, angry. Make us a people with dark brows capable of scaring a few folk. May they look at us and say, "Those guys are so filled with love their anger overflows." AMEN.

In the Aftermath of a Hurricane

Hurricane Fran hit our area of North Carolina on September 6, 1996. Our area was devastated because we usually do not get the full force of hurricanes this far inland. This and the next prayer were on subsequent days when classes resumed after the hurricane.

OK, GOD, Job-like, we feel enough is enough. Is a hurricane Behemoth? What are we to say to you: Are you in a hurricane? We fear acknowledging that you may be. We want to protect you. We want to think you and your creation are benign. The result, of course, is to rob you of your creation. The hurricane becomes "just nature," but "just nature" cannot be your creation. Do we dare believe that Christ could still the winds? We want our world regular, predictable, not subject to disorder or chaos. So if you are in the hurricane, please just butt out.

We confess we have lost the skill to see you in

your creation. We pray to you to care for the injured, those in shock, those without housing, those in despair, but how can you do so if you are not in the hurricane? We confess we do not know how to put this together. We want you to heal our hurts, but we really do not want to think you can. We want to think you make it possible for us to help one another, but it is not clear why we think we need your help. Help us to call for help. AMEN.

Neighbors in Pain

GOD, give us Jobian humility. Help us stand awestruck—silent—before the mystery of your creation. Help us understand the wildness of your creation, wildness at once as terrible as it is beautiful. Help us see you in the terror and the beauty, knowing as we do the agony of our sin in your life. We have seen that agony in your Son's cross. We know his agony continues still so that our unbelief might not damn us. Help us claim to be Christ for one another, defeating the loneliness in which sin cannot help but clothe us. So freed, make us neighbors for one another. In the pain, in our fear of being out of control, may we discover our ability to need help and in that discovery be enabled to help others. We know normality will quickly return and we will again be OK, not needing anyone else. But sear into our memories the moments when we discern we are not our own and, thus, come close to perfection. AMEN.

Memory and Pain

CRUCIFIED LORD, your creation is full of pain. Our lives are filled with pain. We must appear happy, to be OK, to others and ourselves. After all, we know no one likes to be around people in pain. So we cannot even be around ourselves. We refuse to remember because memory is just another name for pain—dull, meaningless pain that makes us numb. But you would have us be a passionate people, filled with the Spirit, possessed by memory. We fear that if we remember, the pain will return and kill our present. Give us courage, which is just another name for friends, to stare down the terror in our own and our neighbors' lives, that we may be your joyous people. AMEN.

Save Us from Our American Power

I wrote this prayer after the United States sent missiles into Iraq because Iraq had allegedly tried to kill George Bush when he visited Kuwait. President Clinton showed he "meant business" by bombing them.

GRACEFUL LORD, we find ourselves living in the most powerful country in the world. The pride and self-righteousness such power breeds are beyond compare. No power exists that can humble us. We are tyrants of all we survey. We decide to bomb these people, send rockets against those people, kill those we call terrorists—all because we can. We are the most powerful people in the world. It is hard not to be caught up in such power. It is intoxicating. Save us from it. Sober us with the knowledge that you will judge this nation, you will humble this nation, you will destroy this nation for our pride. Send us a reminder that you are God, that you alone have the right of vengeance, and if it be your will, make those we bomb instruments of your judgment. At the very least, save us from the "normality of killing." AMEN.

Neglected Gifts

THE BEAUTY OF a green leaf turning red, the brightness of a stranger's face, the joy of a cat at play, the sheer wonder coming from the generosity of friends—for all this and so much more we give you thanks, we praise you, gifting God. Help us remember, however, that you have made us, through Jesus Christ, your thanksgiving sacrifice for a world that refuses to acknowledge its giftedness. Let us rush again and again to your feast of the new age, where you provide the space and time for us to enjoy being your joy. AMEN.

Make Us the Memory of Your World

TIMELY GOD, we would forget you if we could. Remembering is hateful for us. We look back on our lives and so often all we see is our smallness, our need to force others to recognize us, the pettiness of our sins. But in our desire to forget you, we forget ourselves, becoming no one who lives nowhere. Thank God, you force us to live in your time, capable of memory even of our sins now healed—reconciled even to our past, ourselves, through the gift of confession. Make us remember, and in such remembering make us your memory for the world. AMEN.

The Too-Different, Too-Near God

AWESOME LORD, you will forgive us if we prefer you just a bit more familiar. We are sure you do not mean to frighten us, but distance and difference can be unsettling. We love the Grand Canyon but prefer not to get too close to the rim. Come to us, but be less dramatic. We have all the drama we can stand just getting through the day. So we dread how you come to us this and every day— crucified. We stand speechless before the majesty of your cross. Frightened yet attracted. How unexpected to learn the awesome distance between you and us by your nearness. AMEN.

Part Three
ENDINGS

Fearing God More Than Death

Margaret was a student at Duke whose husband died of a chronic illness.

LORD OF LIFE, death scares us. We know we must die, but we have become skilled at living in a manner that ignores that stubborn fact. After all, most of us are not really old enough yet to have to face our deaths. Death happens to the old, not us, who are thus condemned to live as if we are perpetually young. Yet death slinks even into our young lives. We do not like it. We try to hide its presence by not being present to those dying and avoiding those who must be present to the dying. We therefore pray for your unfailing and sustaining presence for Margaret as she today buries her husband. Give her the same courage that sustained her and him through his illness. May that same courage find a home in our lives, that we may come to fear you more than our own deaths and thus be enabled to be present to one another. AMEN.

Facing Down the Kingdom of Death

LORD OF DEATH and Lord of life, we live as if we will not die and, so living, live deadly lives. Save us from this living death by engrafting us into your kingdom of life. As people of that kingdom we name now all those recent dead to your care—Brian, Catherine, Stuart. We look forward to the fellowship of the communion of the saints and pray for those friends to sustain us for the facing down of the kingdom of death. AMEN.

Enliven Our Clichés

Professor McClintock Fulkerson is my colleague on the faculty of the divinity school. Her mother died in 1997, rather unexpectedly.

DEAR LORD, death comes and goes, touching those we know and do not know. A sobering reality. Mary McClintock Fulkerson's mother is among those recently dead. Help us be present to Mary and her family so that the sadness of death will not overwhelm. May the formulas we use at such times—"I am so sorry to hear about your mother"—be made more than clichés, by making us your presence. We are, after all, your baptized people. Give us the power to remember our baptism as those we love die. AMEN.

Fleshly God . . .

FLESHLY GOD, you greet us with bodily presence
and thus make it impossible for us to control you.
We give thanks for our bodies, destined as they are
to death. Through them you give us life. Make us
your resurrection body, that the world may know
your Spirit. AMEN.

A Heart That Beat to the Rhythms of Grace

Professor Frederick Herzog taught systematic theology in the divinity school at Duke for many years. He was a fierce advocate for the poor, being among the first to take liberation theology seriously. He died on October 9, 1995, in a faculty meeting.

DEAR JESUS, we have been taught that your heart is the life of us all. We pray, therefore, for you to continue to care for your servant Fred Herzog, whose heart was great and good. We need such goodness, for without it we die. His good heart beat weirdly, which is not surprising since his heart always beat to the rhythms of your grace. He was no doubt ready to die, and we must now let him loose. We ask you to heal our hearts, so that his life may continue to be a balm for us all. AMEN.

Two Tough Saints

On the occasion of Mother Teresa's death.

SANCTIFYING LORD, we praise you for sending us your saints. Hard people. They do not make life easy. We want them to be sanctimonious, to be pedestal people, as different as possible. Not our kind. Unworldly. But instead they are hard. They will not let us alone. "Do not kill, especially in war." "Do not abort." "Do not abandon the poor, the sick, the old in the name of compassion," she said. Dorothy Day said. Mother Teresa said. God, these women were tough as tanned rawhide. Not very attractive. But I guess we do not get to choose whom you choose. So we pray you enjoy these strange women who are now enjoying that communion where the poor are fed and clothed. Thank you for sending us these glimpses, these tastes of heaven. AMEN.

On the Death of Henri Nouwen

Father Henri Nouwen was a Catholic priest, spiritual director and writer of extraordinary power. He had become the chaplain at Daybreak, which is the L'Arche home for the mentally handicapped in Toronto. He died in 1996.

LORD OF LIFE, Lord of death, we give you thanks for the life, the ministry, the witness of Father Henri M. Nouwen. His life was constituted by words, but he longed for silence. You have now constituted him by your eloquent silence, by naming him a member of that chorus called the communion of saints. We pray for his friends at Daybreak, who will rightly feel the silence of his death as loss. May they look into one another's faces and see your unfailing presence. So seeing, may they rejoice in the life of this strange man, who so willingly exposed his life so that we might rejoice in the life you have given us. AMEN.

A Prayer for the Situation Ethicist in the Ultimate Situation

In 1996 Joseph Fletcher wrote Situation Ethics, *a book I often criticized. He lived long (over ninety years) and wrote much that I continue to criticize. He died in 1996.*

LORD OF DEATH AND LIFE, we commend to you your strange servant Joseph Fletcher. He reminded us that Christians are nothing if we are not love. He challenged our legalism and self-righteousness. Now that he is in the ultimate "situation," may he be joined with those in the communion of saints who share that activity that alone is perfection, who sing your praise. Be with us who are left singing imperfectly, that we may at least get some of the notes right. AMEN.

On the Death of a Cat

Tuck was a Siamese cat who lived twenty years. I loved him dearly, but Paula, my wife, and he had a "special" relationship. The last year of his life involved transfusions of water that he calmly endured. He died on October 17, 1996.

PASSIONATE LORD, by becoming one of us, you revealed your unrelenting desire to have us love you. As we were created for such love, you have made us to love your creation and through such love, such desire, learn to love you. We believe every love we have you have given us. Tuck's love of us, and our love of him, is a beacon, a participation, in your love of all your creation. We thank you, we sing your praise, for the wonderful life of this cat. His calm, his dignity, his courage, his humor, his needs, his patience, his always "being there," made us better, made our love for one another better, made us better love you. We will miss him. Help us not fear remembering him, confident that the sadness such memory brings is bounded by the joy that Tuck existed and, with us, is part of your glorious creation, a harbinger of your peaceable kingdom. AMEN.

The Terror in Our Neighbors' Lives

On the occasion of the suicide of a divinity school student.

DEAR GOD, we do not desire to know the terror in our neighbors' lives. We do not desire to know the terror in our own lives. We live as if we have nothing to fear, and thus we are captivated by fear. May your love overcome our fears so that we can reach out to one another, fearing neither ourselves, others, nor you. We pray for your mercy for those who have killed themselves. We know not their fears, and we thus fear they died alone. They are now yours: in that is our comfort. Comfort all who love them and who will miss their presence. We feel helpless, but praying helps. Thank you for the gift of prayer. AMEN.

Help Us Name Our Lives as Gifts

LORD OF DEATH AND LIFE, help us find our life in you so that we might be free from our fear of death. Our deaths have died in the death of your Son so that, like him, we might rise to life made perfect by your love. Help us name our lives as gifts so we will not jealously try to ensure, through coercion and violence, the regard and envy of others. For we fear without such notice we will not be, we will be dead. Such a living is not joy, and we know we were created for joy and life. Let us therefore learn to live as gifts so that others might rejoice in our existence. AMEN.

Surprised by Hope

I offer this prayer in thanks to the graduate students who assist in the course. They run seminar sessions as well as grade papers and exams. There are many names not named because they change from year to year. I am the most fortunate of people to be claimed by such wonderfully talented and thoughtful people, who make me a better teacher than I would be on my own.

GRACIOUS GOD, you alone have the power to turn our despair into hope. Thank you for giving us people of hope. They are surprises, but they are here. When I think of the richness of your kingdom, I feel unworthy even to claim to be your servant—but then you send the Kathys, Johns, Mikes, and Davids, Kellys, Lauras, Gails, Chrises, and they make me—and us—better than I had hoped. I am never sure I believe or understand all I think, and thus how can I teach? But it happens, and for that I am grateful and humbled. Thank God this semester is almost over. May it, through your grace, never end. AMEN.

Truth Deeper Than Our Violence

LORD OF ALL TIME AND SPACE, we come to the end of this course grateful for the time and space you gave us together. For you all endings are but beginnings. We ask you therefore to make more of this time than we can imagine. You make our past more than we knew and our future full of surprises—and then our present is wonderful joy. May that joy stand as an alternative to the world's despair, so that the world might know that your truth is deeper than our violence. AMEN.

We Know Only As We Are Known

SUSTAINER OF ALL LIFE, infuse our lives with the joy of your Spirit. We know only as we are known. Illumine our lives with knowledge of you, that we may see that our endings are beginnings. Wrench our closings open so that we will not fear suffering, and so learn that it is only through our suffering that you make us your agents. Compel us, make us free so that we manifest the joy of friendship with you and one another. AMEN.